Best Knock-Knock Book Ever

Charles Keller

Illustrated by Jeff Sinclair

SCHOLASTIC INC.

New York Toronto London Auckland Sydney
Mexico City New Delhi Hong Kong Buenos Aires

To Gabriel and Bowen

I would like to acknowledge the help of Stephen Blance, Marcus
Bocchino, Rhoda Crispell, and Brenda Gordon

ISBN 0-439-40128-3

12 11   4 5 6 7/0

Printed in the U.S.A.   23

First Scholastic printing, March 2002

Contents

Knock-knock.
Who's there?
Aaron.
Aaron who?
Aaron all the way home.

Knock-knock.
Who's there?
Abbot.
Abbot who?
Abbot time we eat, isn't it?

Knock-knock.
Who's there?
Abe Lincoln.
Abe Lincoln who?
Abe Lincoln break in the strongest chain.

Knock-knock.
  Who's there?
A.C.
  A.C. who?
A.C. come and A.C. go.

Knock-knock.
  Who's there?
Acme.
  Acme who?
If you acme I'll tell you.

Knock-knock.
  Who's there?
Adam.
  Adam who?
Adam up and give me the bill.

Knock-knock.
  Who's there?
Adore.
  Adore who?
Adore is between us.

Knock-knock.
  Who's there?
A.E.
  A.E. who?
A.E. I owe you.

Knock-knock.
Who's there?
Aikido.
Aikido who?
Aikido you not.

Knock-knock.
Who's there?
Alaska.
Alaska who?
Alaska and you ask him.

Knock-knock.
Who's there?
Alex.
Alex who?
Alex plain later.

Knock-knock.
Who's there?
Alfreda.
Alfreda who?
Alfreda the dark.

Knock-knock.
Who's there?
Amarillo.
Amarillo who?
Amarillo-fashioned girl.

Knock-knock.
Who's there?
Amen.
Amen who?
Amen hot water again.

Knock-knock.
Who's there?
Amnesia.
Amnesia who?
Oh, you got it too.

Knock-knock.
Who's there?
Andy.
Andy who?
Andy all lived happily ever after.

Knock-knock.
  Who's there?
Andy.
  Andy who?
Andy music goes on and on.

Knock-knock.
  Who's there?
Anita.
  Anita who?
Anita you like Anita hole in the head.

Knock-knock.
  Who's there?
Anita.
  Anita who?
Anita ride into town.

Knock-knock.
 Who's there?
Anvil.
 Anvil who?
Anvil you be coming too?

Knock-knock.
 Who's there?
Apricot.
 Apricot who?
Apricot my key, open up.

Knock-knock.
 Who's there?
A quorum.
 A quorum who?
A quorum is where I keep my fish.

Knock-knock.
 Who's there?
Arizona.
 Arizona who?
Arizona room for one of us in this town.

Knock-knock.
 Who's there?
Arm.
 Arm who?
Arm always chasing rainbows.

Knock-knock.
Who's there?
Armstrong.
Armstrong who?
Armstrong as an ox.

Knock-knock.
Who's there?
Ash.
Ash who?
Bless you.

Knock-knock.
Who's there?
Asparagus.
Asparagus who?
Asparagus the argument, we don't want to hear it.

Knock-knock.
  Who's there?
Astor.
  Astor who?
Astor what her name is.

Knock-knock.
  Who's there?
Atlas.
  Atlas who?
Atlas I'm here.

Knock-knock.
  Who's there?
Avenue.
  Avenue who?
Avenue heard this joke before?

Knock-knock.
  Who's there?
Babylon.
  Babylon who?
Babylon if you must.

Knock-knock.
  Who's there?
Bella.
  Bella who?
Bella the ball.

Knock-knock.
  Who's there?
Ben and Don.
  Ben and Don who?
Ben there, Don that.

Knock-knock.
  Who's there?
Bernie D.
  Bernie D who?
Bernie D candles at both ends.

Knock-knock.
  Who's there?
Bertha.
  Bertha who?
Bertha the blues.

Knock-knock.
  Who's there:
Bette.
  Bette who?
Bette you can't guess my name.

Knock-knock.
  Who's there?
Blank.
  Blank who?
You're welcome.

Knock-knock.
  Who's there?
Blast.
  Blast who?
Blast, but not least.

Knock-knock.
Who's there?
Bolivia.
Bolivia who?
Bolivia me!

Knock-knock.
Who's there?
Booty.
Booty who?
Booty is only skin deep.

Knock-knock.
Who's there?
Button.
Button who?
Button into what's not your business.

15

Knock-knock.
  Who's there?
Cameron.
  Cameron who?
Cameron over here.

Knock-knock.
  Who's there?
Candace.
  Candace who.
Candace door be opened?

Knock-knock.
  Who's there?
Canoe.
  Canoe who?
Canoe help me with my homework?

Knock-knock.
  Who's there?
Carlo.
  Carlo who?
Carlo on gas.

Knock-knock.
  Who's there?
Casino.
  Casino who?
Casino evil.

Knock-knock.
  Who's there?
Castanet.
  Castanet who?
Castanet in the water to catch fish.

Knock-knock.
  Who's there?
C.D.
  C.D. who?
C.D. forest for the trees.

Knock-knock.
  Who's there?
Censure.
  Censure who?
Censure letters by first class mail.

Knock-knock.
  Who's there?
Cereal.
  Cereal who?
Cereal McCoy.

Knock-knock.
  Who's there?
Chantelle.
  Chantelle who?
Chantelle you anything.

Knock-knock.
  Who's there?
Checker.
  Checker who?
Checker out.

Knock-knock.
  Who's there?
Cheese.
  Cheese who?
Cheese funny that way.

Knock-knock.
  Who's there?
Cindy.
  Cindy who?
Cindy movie, read the book.

Knock-knock.
  Who's there?
Clancy.
  Clancy who?
Clancy where I'm going.

Knock-knock.
  Who's there?
Coma.
  Coma who?
Coma your hair.

Knock-knock.
  Who's there?
Conan.
  Conan who?
Conan the cob.

Knock-knock.
  Who's there?
Conscience stricken.
  Conscience stricken who?
Don't conscience stricken before they hatch.

Knock-knock.
  Who's there?
Cows.
  Cows who?
No, cows moo.

Knock-knock.
  Who's there?
Crate.
  Crate who?
Crate to be here.

Knock-knock.
Who's there?
Crepes.
Crepes who?
Crepes of Wrath.

Knock-knock.
Who's there?
Crimea.
Crimea who?
"Crimea River."

Knock-knock.
Who's there?
Cybil.
Cybil who?
Cybil War.

Knock-knock.
Who's there?
Cypress.
Cypress who?
Cypress your suit.

Knock-knock.
Who's there?
Czar.
Czar who?
Czar she blows!

Knock-knock.
  Who's there?
Dakota.
  Dakota who?
Dakota fits fine, the pants are too long.

Knock-knock.
  Who's there?
Darby.
  Darby who?
Darby stung me.

Knock-knock.
  Who's there?
Darrel.
  Darrel who?
Darrel never be another you.

Knock-knock.
Who's there?
Darwin.
Darwin who?
Darwin young man on the flying trapeze.

Knock-knock.
Who's there?
Dawn.
Dawn who?
Dawn bite off more than you can chew.

Knock-knock.
Who's there?
Debt.
Debt who?
Debt men tell no tales.

Knock-knock.
Who's there?
Dee.
Dee who?
Dee joke's on me.

Knock-knock.
Who's there?
Defense.
Defense who?
Defense keeps the dog in.

Knock-knock.
  Who's there?
Demure.
  Demure who?
Demure you get, Demure you want.

Knock-knock.
  Who's there?
Demure.
  Demure who?
Demure the merrier.

Knock-knock.
  Who's there?
Dennis.
  Dennis who?
Dennis this rain going to stop?

Knock-knock.
  Who's there?
Denver.
  Denver who?
Denver in the world are we?

Knock-knock.
  Who's there?
Depend.
  Depend who?
Depend is mightier than the sword.

Knock-knock.
Who's there?
Derby.
Derby who?
Derby ghosts in that haunted house.

Knock-knock.
Who's there?
Diesel.
Diesel who?
Diesel be your last chance.

Knock-knock.
Who's there?
Dina.
Dina who?
Dina at eight.

Knock-knock.
  Who's there?
Dinosaur.
  Dinosaur who?
Dinosaur at you—you burnt the toast.

Knock-knock.
  Who's there?
Divide.
  Divide who?
Divide world of sports.

Knock-knock.
  Who's there?
Dobie.
  Dobie who?
Dobie cruel to animals.

Knock-knock.
Who's there?
Dole.
Dole who?
Dole truth and nothing but the truth.

Knock-knock.
Who's there?
Don and Greta.
Don and Greta who?
Don and Greta round much any more.

Knock-knock.
Who's there?
Don.
Don who?
Don want to tell you my name.

Knock-knock.
Who's there?
Doughnut.
Doughnut who?
Doughnut thing till you hear from me.

Knock-knock.
Who's there?
Duane.
Duane who?
Duane the bathtub, rubber ducky drowning.

Knock-knock.
Who's there?
Duncan.
Duncan who?
Duncan your doughnut again?

Knock-knock.
Who's there?
Dustin.
Dustin who?
Dustin furniture with polish.

Knock-knock.
Who's there?
Dwight.
Dwight who?
Dwight as rain.

Knock-knock.
Who's there?
Eamon.
Eamon who?
Eamon the mood for love.

Knock-knock.
Who's there?
Eben.
Eben who?
Eben a good girl.

Knock-knock.
Who's there?
Eddy.
Eddy who?
Eddy body got a tissue? I've got a cold.

Knock-knock.
  Who's there?
Effie.
  Effie who?
"Effie Thing's Coming Up Roses."

Knock-knock.
  Who's there?
Eggs.
  Eggs who?
Eggs marks the spot.

Knock-knock.
  Who's there?
Egos.
  Egos who?
Egos wherever he wants to.

Knock-knock.
  Who's there?
Eisenhower.
  Eisenhower who?
Eisenhower late for school.

Knock-knock.
  Who's there?
Elise.
  Elise who?
Elise signed by a tenant.

Knock-knock.
Who's there?
Eliza.
Eliza who?
Eliza lot, so watch your step.

Knock-knock.
Who's there?
Ella Vance.
Ella Vance who?
Ella Vance never forget.

Knock-knock.
Who's there?
Erie.
Erie who?
Erie is, right on time.

Knock-knock.
Who's there?
Eschew.
Eschew who?
Eschew goes on your foot.

Knock-knock.
Who's there?
Estelle.
Estelle who?
Estelle waiting for you to open the door.

Knock-knock.
Who's there?
Etch.
Etch who?
Bless you.

Knock-knock.
Who's there?
Ethan.
Ethan who?
Ethan everything in sight.

Knock-knock.
Who's there?
Eugenes.
Eugenes who?
Eugenes need washing.

Knock-knock.
Who's there?
Europa.
Europa who?
Europa steer and I'll watch.

Knock-knock.
Who's there?
Ewer.
Ewer who?
Ewer getting sleepy.

Knock-knock.
Who's there?
Eyelet.
Eyelet who?
Eyelet you in.

Knock-knock.
Who's there?
Falsetto.
Falsetto who?
Falsetto teeth.

Knock-knock.
Who's there?
Fender.
Fender who?
Fender moon comes over the mountain.

Knock-knock.
Who's there?
Ferdinand.
Ferdinand who?
Ferdinand is worth two in the bush.

34

Knock-knock.
Who's there?
Flea.
Flea who?
"Flea, fie, foh, fum."

Knock-knock.
Who's there?
Florist.
Florist who?
Florist the opposite of ceiling.

Knock-knock.
Who's there?
Flossie.
Flossie who?
Flossie your teeth.

Knock-knock.
Who's there?
Forest.
Forest who?
Forest the eye can see.

Knock-knock.
Who's there?
Fortification.
Fortification who?
Fortification I go to the seashore.

Knock-knock.
Who's there?
Francine.
Francine who?
Francine it all.

Knock-knock.
Who's there?
Frieda.
Frieda who?
"Who's a Frieda the Big Bad Wolf?"

Knock-knock.
Who's there?
Fritz.
Fritz who?
"Fritz a Wonderful Life."

Knock-knock.
  Who's there?
Garter.
  Garter who?
Garter date with an angel.

Knock-knock.
  Who's there?
Gary.
  Gary who?
Gary the package for me.

Knock-knock.
  Who's there?
Gas.
  Gas who?
"Gas Who's Coming to Dinner."

Knock-knock.
Who's there?
G.I.
G.I. who?
G.I. don't know.

Knock-knock.
Who's there?
Gladwin.
Gladwin who?
Gladwin you're leaving.

Knock-knock.
Who's there?
Glove.
Glove who?
"Glove is a Many-Splendored Thing."

Knock-knock.
Who's there?
Goatee.
Goatee who?
Goatee off—the other golfers are waiting.

Knock-knock.
Who's there?
Goosie.
Goosie who?
Goosie who's at the door.

Knock-knock.
  Who's there?
Gouda.
  Gouda who?
Gouda see you again.

Knock-knock.
  Who's there?
Gruesome.
  Gruesome who?
Gruesome tomatoes in my garden.

Knock-knock.
  Who's there?
Gwen.
  Gwen who?
Gwen will I see you again?

Knock-knock.
  Who's there?
Hair combs.
  Hair combs who?
Hair combs the bride.

Knock-knock.
  Who's there?
Half.
  Half who?
Half I got a girl for you.

Knock-knock.
  Who's there?
Hall.
  Hall who?
"Hall the king's horses and hall the king's men."

Knock-knock.
  Who's there?
Hallow.
  Hallow who?
Hallow down there.

Knock-knock.
  Who's there?
Hannibal.
  Hannibal who?
Hannibal in a china shop.

Knock-knock.
  Who's there?
Hans.
  Hans who?
Hans off my computer.

Knock-knock.
  Who's there?
Harpy.
  Harpy who?
Harpy to see you again.

Knock-knock.
  Who's there?
Harris.
  Harris who?
"Harris looking at you, kid."

Knock-knock.
  Who's there?
Harry.
  Harry who?
Harry up, I'm starving.

Knock-knock.
  Who's there?
Harvey.
  Harvey who?
Harvey going to stop meeting like this?

Knock-knock.
  Who's there?
Harvey Gotti.
  Harvey Gotti who?
Harvey Gotti wait here all night?

Knock-knock.
  Who's there?
Heaven.
  Heaven who?
Heaven you heard enough knock-knock jokes?

Knock-knock.
  Who's there?
Hector.
  Hector who?
"Hector halls with boughs of holly."

Knock-knock.
 Who's there?
Hedda.
 Hedda who?
Hedda off at the pass.

Knock-knock.
 Who's there?
Highway cop.
 Highway cop who?
Highway cop at seven every morning.

Knock-knock.
 Who's there?
Hippie.
 Hippie who?
Hippic birthday to you.

CARROT CAKE! ...GROOVY!!

Knock-knock.
  Who's there?
Honor.
  Honor who?
"Honor clear day you can see forever."

Knock-knock.
  Who's there?
Hoover.
  Hoover who?
Hoover you expecting?

Knock-knock.
  Who's there?
Horace.
  Horace who?
Horace and buggy.

Knock-knock.
  Who's there?
House.
  House who?
House business?

Knock-knock.
  Who's there?
Hugh.
  Hugh who?
Hugh who yourself.

Knock-knock.
  Who's there?
Humphrey.
  Humphrey who?
Humphrey ever blowing bubbles.

Knock-knock.
  Who's there?
Hunger.
  Hunger who?
Hunger wash out to dry.

Knock-knock.
  Who's there?
Huron.
  Huron who?
Huron time for once.

Knock-knock.
Who's there?
Ice water.
Ice water who?
Ice water fly with my fly swatter.

Knock-knock.
Who's there?
Ida.
Ida who?
Ida who potato.

Knock-knock.
Who's there?
Imus.
Imus who?
Imus get in out of the rain.

Knock-knock.
Who's there?
India.
India who?
India cool, cool of the evening.

Knock-knock.
Who's there?
Indy.
Indy who?
Indy mood.

Knock-knock.
Who's there?
Iraq.
Iraq who?
Iraq my brain but couldn't get the answer.

Knock-knock.
Who's there?
Irish.
Irish who?
Irish upon a star.

Knock-knock.
  Who's there?
Irma.
  Irma who?
Irma going to sit right down and write myself a
  letter.

Knock-knock.
  Who's there?
Iron.
  Iron who?
Iron joy being a girl.

Knock-knock.
  Who's there?
Isidore.
  Isidore who?
Isidore unlocked?

Knock-knock.
  Who's there?
Israel.
  Israel who?
Israel or fake?

Knock-knock.
  Who's there?
Issue.
  Issue who?
Issue ready to go?

Knock-knock.
  Who's there?
Itzhak.
  Itzhak who?
"Itzhak small world after all."

Knock-knock.
  Who's there?
Ivan.
  Ivan who?
Ivan, you lose.

Knock-knock.
  Who's there?
Jackson.
  Jackson who?
Jackson the box.

Knock-knock.
  Who's there?
Jaws.
  Jaws who?
Jaws till the well runs dry.

Knock-knock.
  Who's there?
Jenny.
  Jenny who?
Jenny a hearing aid? I've been knocking for five
  minutes.

Knock-knock.
Who's there?
Jenny.
Jenny who?
Jenny body home?

Knock-knock.
Who's there?
Jess.
Jess who?
Jess in time.

Knock-knock.
Who's there?
Jewel.
Jewel who?
Jewel be sorry.

Knock-knock.
Who's there?
Jimmy.
Jimmy who?
Jimmy liberty or Jimmy death.

Knock-knock.
Who's there?
Josie.
Josie who?
Josie who's at the door.

Knock-knock.
Who's there?
Jules.
Jules who?
Jules are in the safe.

Knock-knock.
Who's there?
Juliet.
Juliet who?
Juliet the cat out of the bag.

Knock-knock.
Who's there?
Junior.
Junior who?
Junior flowers will come up.

Knock-knock.
Who's there?
Juno.
Juno who?
I don't know, Juno?

Knock-knock.
Who's there?
Jupiter.
Jupiter who?
Jupiter note on my door?

Knock-knock.
Who's there?
Justice.
Justice who?
Justice I got home the phone rang.

Knock-knock.
Who's there?
Justin.
Justin who?
"Justin time, I found you Justin time."

Knock-knock.
  Who's there?
Karaoke.
  Karaoke who?
Karaoke or not okay?

Knock-knock.
  Who's there?
Katmandu.
  Katmandu who?
Katmandu what Catwoman wants.

Knock-knock.
  Who's there?
Kermit.
  Kermit who?
Kermit me to introduce myself.

Knock-knock.
Who's there?
Ketchup.
Ketchup who?
Ketchup with her before she gets away.

Knock-knock.
Who's there?
Kip.
Kip who?
Kip your sunny side up.

Knock-knock.
Who's there?
Knoxville.
Knoxville who?
Knoxville get you an answer if you wait long enough.

Knock-knock.
Who's there?
Koala-T.
Koala-T who?
Koala-T knock-knocks are hard to find.

Knock-knock.
Who's there?
Kokomo.
Kokomo who?
Kokomo food—I'm hungry.

Knock-knock.
Who's there?
Land.
Land who?
It's "land-ho," not "land who."

Knock-knock.
Who's there?
Levin.
Levin who?
"Levin on a jet plane."

Knock-knock.
Who's there?
Leopold.
Leopold who?
Leopold the class and everyone wants a new teacher.

Knock-knock.
  Who's there?
Letter.
  Letter who?
Letter smile be your umbrella.

Knock-knock.
  Who's there?
Lice.
  Lice who?
Lice out by ten o'clock.

Knock-knock.
  Who's there?
Lilac.
  Lilac who?
Lilac that and you'll get punished.

Knock-knock.
  Who's there?
Liv.
  Liv who?
Liv no stone unturned.

Knock-knock.
  Who's there?
Liver.
  Liver who?
Liver round here?

Knock-knock.
Who's there?
Macon.
Macon who?
"Macon a list, checking it twice."

Knock-knock.
Who's there?
Macon.
Macon who?
Macon whoopie.

Knock-knock.
Who's there?
Major.
Major who?
Major bed, now lie in it.

Knock-knock.
Who's there?
Mandalay.
Mandalay who?
Mandalay the kitchen tiles.

Knock-knock.
Who's there?
Massachusetts.
Massachusetts who?
Massachusetts is what you hear when a train blows
    its whistle.

Knock-knock.
Who's there?
Mayonnaise.
Mayonnaise who?
"Mayonnaise be merry and bright..."

Knock-knock.
Who's there?
Melissa.
Melissa who?
Melissa longer than your list.

Knock-knock.
  Who's there?
Me.
  Me who?
Meow.

Knock-knock.
  Who's there?
Menu.
  Menu who?
Menu stay here, women over there.

Knock-knock.
  Who's there?
Michigan.
  Michigan who?
"Michigan," said the batter after the third strike.

Knock-knock.
  Who's there?
Midas.
  Midas who?
Midas well open up, I'm not going away.

Knock-knock.
  Who's there?
Mira.
  Mira who?
Mira, Mira, on the wall.

Knock-knock.
Who's there?
Monet.
Monet who?
Monet burns a hole in my pocket.

Knock-knock.
Who's there?
Moose.
Moose who?
Moose beautiful girl in the world.

Knock-knock.
Who's there?
Mustard.
Mustard who?
Mustard been a beautiful baby.

Knock-knock.
Who's there?
Nathan.
Nathan who?
Nathan to lose.

Knock-knock.
Who's there?
Nestor.
Nestor who?
Nestor lives my neighbor.

Knock-knock.
Who's there?
Newark.
Newark who?
Newark for Noah.

Knock-knock.
Who's there?
Newark.
Newark who?
Newark keeps piling up.

Knock-knock.
Who's there?
Noggin.
Noggin who?
Noggin at your door.

Knock-knock.
Who's there?
Notify.
Notify who?
Notify can help it.

Knock-knock.
Who's there?
Nova.
Nova who?
Nova look back.

Knock-knock.
Who's there?
O. A.
O. A. who?
"O. A. down South in Dixie."

Knock-knock.
Who's there?
Occult.
Occult who?
Occult in my nose.

Knock-knock.
Who's there?
Ocelot.
Ocelot who?
Ocelot of money for that.

Knock-knock.
  Who's there?
Ohio.
  Ohio who?
Ohio than the highest mountain.

Knock-knock.
  Who's there?
Oil well.
  Oil well who?
Oil well that ends well.

Knock-knock.
  Who's there?
Oklahoma.
  Oklahoma who?
Oklahoma and wash your face.

Knock-knock.
  Who's there?
Olaf.
  Olaf who?
"Olaf My Heart in San Francisco."

Knock-knock.
  Who's there?
One door.
  One door who?
One door where you are tonight.

Knock-knock.
  Who's there?
Opel.
  Opel who?
Opel of mine.

Knock-knock.
  Who's there?
Orange shoe.
  Orange shoe who?
Orange shoe going to let me in?

Knock-knock.
  Who's there?
Oregon.
  Oregon who?
Oregon and I'm not coming back.

Knock-knock.
  Who's there?
Orson.
  Orson who?
Orson buggy—want a ride?

Knock-knock.
  Who's there?
Osborne.
  Osborne who?
Osborne in the hospital.

Knock-knock.
Who's there?
Osgood.
Osgood who?
Osgood as it gets.

Knock-knock.
Who's there?
Oslo.
Oslo who?
Oslo down, you're going too fast.

Knock-knock.
Who's there?
Oswego.
Oswego who?
"Oswego into the wild blue yonder."

Knock-knock.
Who's there?
Otter.
Otter who?
Otter apologize for these bad jokes.

Knock-knock.
Who's there?
O. Verdi.
O. Verdi who?
"O. Verdi Rainbow."

Knock-knock.
Who's there?
Owls.
Owls who?
You got it right this time.

Knock-knock.
Who's there?
Paddy.
Paddy who?
Paddy your own canoe.

Knock-knock.
Who's there?
Pakistan.
Pakistan who?
Pakistan lunch. He's working late.

Knock-knock.
Who's there?
Pasadena.
Pasadena who?
Stop when you Pasadena—I'm hungry.

Knock-knock.
Who's there?
Pasteurize.
Pasteurize who?
Pasteurize and over the gums, look out stomach,
here it comes.

Knock-knock.
Who's there?
Patella.
Patella who?
Patella story before bedtime.

Knock-knock.
Who's there?
Paula.
Paula who?
Paula few strings for me.

Knock-knock.
Who's there?
Pawtucket.
Pawtucket who?
I had a dollar, but Pawtucket.

Knock-knock.
Who's there?
Pay cents.
Pay cents who?
Pay cents is a virtue.

Knock-knock.
Who's there?
Peekaboo.
Peekaboo who?
Peekaboo live in glass houses shouldn't throw stones.

Knock-knock.
Who's there?
Peking.
Peking who?
Peking is not allowed.

Knock-knock.
Who's there?
Pembroke.
Pembroke who?
Pembroke, can I use yours?

Knock-knock.
Who's there?
Picture.
Picture who?
Picture favorite flowers.

Knock-knock.
Who's there?
Plate.
Plate who?
"Plate again, Sam."

Knock-knock.
Who's there?
Poker.
Poker who?
Poker Hontas.

Knock-knock.
Who's there?
Poland.
Poland who?
Poland or rich country?

Knock-knock.
Who's there?
Quaint.
Quaint who?
"Quaint nothing but a hound dog."

Knock-knock.
Who's there?
Quake.
Quake who?
Quake up, you sleepyhead.

Knock-knock.
Who's there?
Que Sarah.
Que Sarah who?
"Que Sarah, Sarah; whatever will be, will be."

Knock-knock.
Who's there?
Radio.
Radio who?
Radio not, here I come.

Knock-knock.
Who's there?
Randy and Vanna.
Randy and Vanna who?
Randy race and Vanna medal.

Knock-knock.
Who's there?
Raptor.
Raptor who?
Raptor presents before Christmas.

Knock-knock.
Who's there?
Rhoda.
Rhoda who?
Rhoda dendron.

Knock-knock.
Who's there?
Rich.
Rich who?
Rich way did he go?

Knock-knock.
Who's there?
Robin.
Robin who?
Robin you! Hand over your money!

Knock-knock.
Who's there?
Roger.
Roger who?
Roger. Over and out.

Knock-knock.
Who's there?
Rubber.
Rubber who?
Rubber the wrong way and she'll smack you.

THISSSSSSS KNOCK-KNOCK BOOK ISSSS SSOMETHING SSSPECIAL!!

Knock-knock.
Who's there?
Safari.
Safari who?
Safari so good.

Knock-knock.
Who's there?
Salome.
Salome who?
Salome on rye with mustard.

Knock-knock.
Who's there?
Sarah.
Sarah who?
Sarah doorbell around here? I'm tired of knocking.

Knock-knock.
  Who's there?
Sarasota.
  Sarasota who?
Sarasota in the fridge? I'm thirsty.

Knock-knock.
  Who's there?
Sari.
  Sari who?
Sari, wrong number.

Knock-knock.
  Who's there?
Sauna.
  Sauna who?
"Sauna clear day you can see forever."

Knock-knock.
  Who's there?
Schenectady.
  Schenectady who?
Schenectady plug to the socket.

Knock-knock.
  Who's there?
Scissors.
  Scissors who?
Scissors lovely way to spend the evening.

Knock-knock.
Who's there?
Sedimentary.
Sedimentary who?
Sedimentary, my dear Watson.

Knock-knock.
Who's there?
Serbia.
Serbia who?
Serbia yourself.

Knock-knock.
Who's there?
Sew.
Sew who?
Sew what else is new?

Knock-knock.
Who's there?
Shirley.
Shirley who?
Shirley you know my name.

Knock-knock.
Who's there?
Simmer.
Simmer who?
"Simmer time and the living is easy."

Knock-knock.
Who's there?
Singaporc.
Singapore who?
Singapore song or a rich song.

Knock-knock.
Who's there?
Sizzle.
Sizzle who?
Sizzle be my shining hour.

Knock-knock.
Who's there?
Slater.
Slater who?
Slater than you think.

Knock-knock.
Who's there?
Snow.
Snow who?
Snow use using the doorbell, it's broken.

Knock-knock.
Who's there?
Stan.
Stan who?
Stan up and be counted.

Knock-knock.
Who's there?
Stark.
Stark who?
Stark in here, turn on the light.

Knock-knock.
  Who's there?
Statue.
  Statue who?
Statue in there?

Knock-knock.
  Who's there?
Stephen.
  Stephen who?
Stephen out with my baby.

Knock-knock.
  Who's there?
Stephen.
  Stephen who?
Stephen the gas.

Knock-knock.
  Who's there?
Stu.
  Stu who?
Stu darn hot.

Knock-knock.
  Who's there?
Stu.
  Stu who?
Stu late now.

Knock-knock.
   Who's there?
Tanya.
   Tanya who?
Tanya come out and play?

Knock-knock.
   Who's there?
Tara.
   Tara who?
"Tara-ra-boom-ti-ay."

Knock-knock.
   Who's there?
Tarragon.
   Tarragon who?
Tarragon with the wind.

Knock-knock.
  Who's there?
Tarzan.
  Tarzan who?
Tarzan feather 'em.

Knock-knock.
  Who's there?
Taylor.
  Taylor who?
Taylor I can't make it.

Knock-knock.
  Who's there?
Thayer.
  Thayer who?
Thayer sorry or I'm leaving.

Knock-knock.
  Who's there?
Thee.
  Thee who?
Thee old gray mare.

Knock-knock.
  Who's there?
Theresa.
  Theresa who?
Theresa crowd.

Knock-knock.
  Who's there?
Thistle.
  Thistle who?
Thistle teach you not to ask silly questions.

Knock-knock.
  Who's there?
Tissue.
  Tissue who?
Tissue were here.

Knock-knock.
  Who's there?
Titus.
  Titus who?
Titus a drum.

Knock-knock.
Who's there?
Tobacco.
Tobacco who?
Tobacco your car you have to put it in reverse.

Knock-knock.
Who's there?
Toby.
Toby who?
Toby continued.

Knock-knock.
Who's there?
Tobias.
Tobias who?
Tobias you need a lot of money.

Knock-knock.
Who's there?
Toothache.
Toothache who?
Toothache the high road and I'll take the low road.

Knock-knock.
Who's there?
T. Rex.
T. Rex who?
T. Rex your appetite more than coffee.

Knock-knock.
   Who's there?
Turnip.
   Turnip who?
Turnip the volume. I can't hear.

Knock-knock.
   Who's there?
Twain.
   Twain who?
Twain on track nine.

Knock-knock.
   Who's there?
Typhoid.
   Typhoid who?
Typhoid you were looking for me.

Knock-knock.
Who's there?
Uma.
Uma who?
"Uma Darling Clementine."

Knock-knock.
Who's there?
Upton.
Upton who?
Upton Sesame.

Knock-knock.
Who's there?
U-turn.
U-turn who?
U-turn my legs to jelly.

Knock-knock.
Who's there?
Vanna.
Vanna who?
Vanna go to the movies?

Knock-knock.
Who's there?
Verdi.
Verdi who?
Verdi wave goes, so goes the surfer.

Knock-knock.
Who's there?
Vi.
Vi who?
"Vi do fools fall in love?"

Knock-knock.
Who's there?
Waiter.
Waiter who?
"Waiter till the sun shines, Nellie."

Knock-knock.
Who's there?
Waiver.
Waiver who?
Waiver hands in the air.

Knock-knock.
Who's there?
Wanda.
Wanda who?
Wanda tell me the password? It's cold out here.

Knock-knock.
Who's there?
Wanda Witch.
Wanda Witch who?
Wanda Witch you a Merry Christmas.

Knock-knock.
Who's there?
Weevil.
Weevil who?
Weevil meet again.

Knock-knock.
Who's there?
Wiener.
Wiener who?
Wiener and still champion.

Knock-knock.
Who's there?
West Point.
West Point who?
West Point are you trying to make?

Knock-knock.
Who's there?
Wok.
Wok who?
Wok, don't run.

Knock-knock.
Who's there?
Woody.
Woody who?
Woody want me to say?

Knock-knock.
Who's there?
Woolly.
Woolly who?
Woolly win the race?

Knock-knock.
Who's there?
Wyatt.
Wyatt who?
Wyatt always pours when it rains?

Knock-knock.
Who's there?
Xena.
Xena who?
Xena picture in the paper.

Knock-knock.
Who's there?
Yale.
Yale who?
"Yale, Caesar."

Knock-knock.
Who's there?
Yawl.
Yawl who?
Yawl come back, you hear.

Knock-knock.
  Who's there?
Yoda.
  Yoda who?
Yoda smart one, you tell me.

Knock-knock.
  Who's there?
Yoga.
  Yoga who?
Yoga your way, I'll go mine.

Knock-knock.
  Who's there?
Your sister.
  Your sister who?
You mean you don't know me?

Knock-knock.
  Who's there?
Yukon.
  Yukon who?
Yukon win 'em all.

Knock-knock.
  Who's there?
Zachery.
  Zachery who?
Zachery what I want for Christmas.

Knock-knock.
  Who's there?
Zeal.
  Zeal who?
Zeal it with a kiss.

Knock-knock.
  Who's there?
Zest.
  Zest who?
Zest things in life are free.

Knock-knock.
Who's there?
Zinc.
Zinc who?
Zinc like the Titanic.

Knock-knock.
Who's there?
Zoophyte.
Zoophyte who?
Zoophyte anyone who bothers the animals.

Knock-knock.
Who's there?
Zymosis.
Zymosis who?
Zymosis come back with the Ten Commandments?

Knock-knock.
Who's there?
Zone.
Zone who?
Zone worst enemy.

Index